DATE DUE

Seasonal Crafts

Summer

Gillian Chapman

RSVP

RAINTREE
STECK-VAUGHN
P U B L I S H E R S
The Steck-Vaughn Company

Austin, Texas

Seasonal Crafts

Spring • Summer • Autumn • Winter

Published by Raintree Steck-Vaughn Publishers, an imprint of Steck-Vaughn Company.

Picture acknowledgments:
Axiom 8; Greg Evans 4; Eye Ubiquitous 14 (J.Hulme), 18 (Frank Leather); HAGA/Britstock– IFA 12, 20; Robert Harding Picture Library 6 (Andrew Robinson), 28 (Andy Williams); The Hutchison Library 22 (Liba Taylor); Image Bank 10; Impact 26 (Alain Evrard); Christine Osbourne Pictures 24; ZefaPicture Library 16. Cover photograph by Chris Fairclough. All other commissioned photography by Zul Mukhida. Props made by Gillian Chapman.

Library of Congress Cataloging-in-Publication Data
Chapman, Gillian.
Summer / Gillian Chapman.
    p.   cm.—(Seasonal crafts)
Includes bibliographical references and index.
Summary: Describes some of the holidays that are celebrated around the world in summer, including May Day, Kodomonohi, Flag Day, and South American street festivals, and provides instructions for a variety of related craft projects.
ISBN 0-8172-4873-0
1. Summer festivals—Juvenile literature. [1. Handicraft. 2. Summer festivals. 3. Festivals. 4. Holidays] I. Title. II. Series: Chapman, Gillian. Seasonal Crafts.
GT4505.C55   1998
394.263—dc21   97-17160
                            CIP
                            AC

Printed in Italy. Bound in the United States.
1 2 3 4 5 6 7 8 9 0 02 01 00 99 98

Contents

Words that are shown in **bold** are explained in the glossary on page 31.

Summertime

△ *Ice cream is very popular, especially for cooling off in the summer.*

In many countries summertime is the season of warmth and growth. People take their vacations, enjoy days off in the country, and relax in the sunshine. Traditionally many of the holidays and events of this season are celebrated outdoors.

Summer is a happy time. Flowers make splashes of color everywhere, and people tend to wear colorful clothes that suit the cheerful, sunny weather.

Summer Projects

All the projects featured in this book reflect the season of summer, with its warm sunshine and bright colors. Some of the projects are practical as well as fun to make. You can play with some of them —and even wear others!

Before you start:
Get all the materials and equipment you need before you start a project. They are listed at the top of each page. You may want to ask an adult to help with some of the steps.

Summer Color

Summer flowers and butterflies give us plenty of ideas for color schemes and designs. It is a great time to take a sketch pad and pencil outside and draw. Look carefully at the petals and leaves of different flowers, and record your findings.

Bring your notes inside and use them in your project work. Try to use the colors and shapes you have observed when you design a flower hat, some snazzy sunglasses, or a sunflower mosaic.

May Day

△ *Dancing around the maypole is a very old May Day tradition.*

May Day, falling on the first day of May, is a spring holiday that has been celebrated for thousands of years. The **Celts** held a May Day festival called **Beltane** and lit bonfires. They believed the heat from the fires would help the sun become powerful and warm again.

It has traditionally been a holiday associated with dancing and processions. In some places it is the custom to crown a May queen with flowers and dance with ribbons around the maypole. In some countries May Day is also known as Labor Day and is celebrated with **political** rallies and parades.

Making Flower Hats

1 Use the compass to draw a $5\frac{1}{2}$ in. diameter circle in the center of a piece of poster board. ▽

You will need:
* A piece of colored poster board
* Pencil and ruler
* A compass
* Pencil and ruler
* Glue
* $5\frac{1}{2}$ in. green felt circle
* 24 in. green ribbon
* Scissors
* Tissue paper

2 Draw a circle of large petals around the inner circle, and cut out the flower shape carefully. △

4 Turn the flower over. Cut out some more paper petals, and stick them to the flower, so they overlap each other. ▽

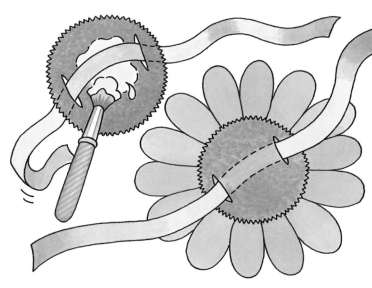

3 Cut two slits in the felt circle, and thread the ribbon through. Attach the ribbon to the felt with glue. Then glue the felt circle to the center of the flower. △

5 Decorate the center of the flower by sticking on small pieces of crumpled tissue paper. △

Wesak

Wesak, the Buddhist Festival of Light, takes place in either May or June, depending on when the moon is full. It celebrates the birth, **enlightenment,** and death of the Buddha, which some Buddhists believe occurred in one day. It is a festival of great happiness and joy.

People burn lanterns, candles, and incense in Buddhist temples and shrines as symbols of the Buddha's enlightenment.

*During Wesak **captive** birds are freed as a symbol of the love the Buddha showed to all living creatures.* ▽

Making Moving Animals

You will need:
* Construction paper
* Pencil
* Scissors
* Hole punch
* Paper fasteners
* Markers
* Thin elastic cord

1 Sketch a simple animal shape on the paper. You may choose a bird, a fish, or an animal. Think about the parts of the animal that move, like the legs and tail, and draw these separately. ▽

2 Color in all the pieces and cut them out. Then assemble them into the basic animal shape. △

3 Use the hole punch to make holes in the pieces and body at the points where they meet. Then join them together with the paper fasteners. △

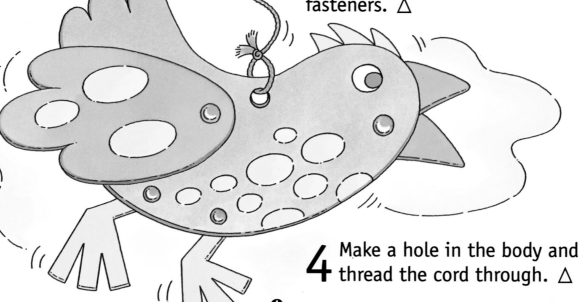

4 Make a hole in the body and thread the cord through. △

Tangonosekku

△ *The skies are filled with carp streamers at Tangonosekku.*

Tangonosekku is a Japanese Boys' Festival that was traditionally a day when all the boys in a family are **honored**. In recent years the festival has been renamed Kodomonohi, or Children's Day, and all children are honored.

The carp is a symbol of strength and bravery, qualities that the boys tried to learn. Carp-shaped paper kites and streamers are flown from the rooftops of homes where the boys live. The largest and most beautiful kite represented the oldest boy.

Making a Swimming Fish

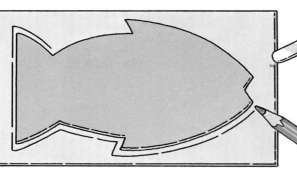

You will need:
* Pieces of paper
* Pencil
* Scissors
* Markers
* Plant stick
* Double-sided tape
* Glue stick

1 Sketch the fish shape onto paper and cut it out. Then use the shape as a pattern to cut out an identical shape. △

2 Fold one of the fish shapes in half, and cut some slits along the side. Do the same with the second fish. △

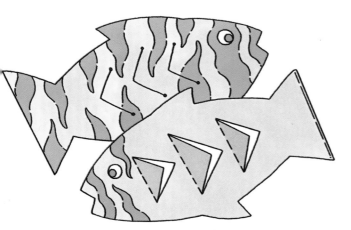

3 Flatten the fish shapes and decorate them with colored markers. Fold back the cutout slots to make the fins. △

4 Tape the plant stick to the back of one of the shapes, using the double-sided tape. Place the second shape over the top, so the stick is secure inside. △

5 Place the stick in the ground and watch the fish move with the wind. ▽

11

Flag Day & Independence Day

These two important days in the American calendar both occur during the summer. Flag Day is held on June 14 and remembers the day in 1777 when Congress **adopted** the first flag. It had 13 white and red stripes and 13 stars, each representing the **original** states. As more states joined the union, extra stars were added.

The Declaration of Independence was signed in 1776 on July 4. The day is celebrated with fireworks and parades.

In New Orleans the "Stars and Stripes" are everywhere in this Fourth of July parade. ▽

Making Pennants & Badges

You can make pennants and badges to celebrate a special day. Everyone enjoys waving pennants and wearing badges, so make plenty and design them to suit the occasion.

You will need:
* Construction paper
* A compass
* Scissors and ruler
* Colored markers
* Tape
* Plant sticks
* Large safety pins

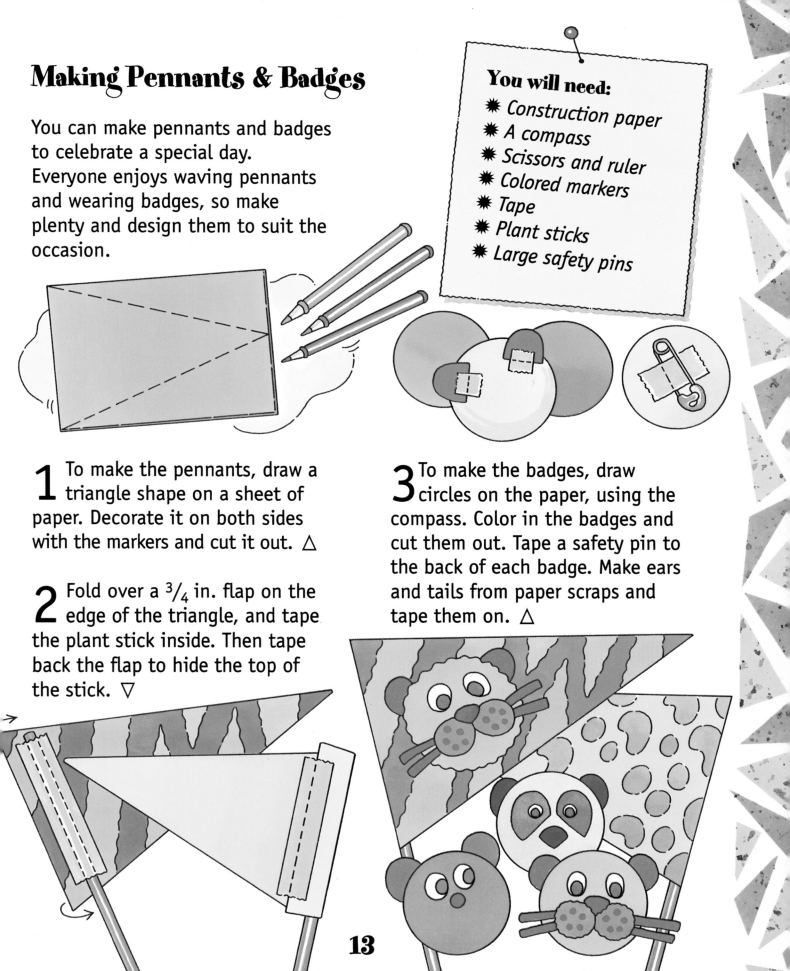

1 To make the pennants, draw a triangle shape on a sheet of paper. Decorate it on both sides with the markers and cut it out. △

2 Fold over a 3/4 in. flap on the edge of the triangle, and tape the plant stick inside. Then tape back the flap to hide the top of the stick. ▽

3 To make the badges, draw circles on the paper, using the compass. Color in the badges and cut them out. Tape a safety pin to the back of each badge. Make ears and tails from paper scraps and tape them on. △

Dragon Boat Festival

△ *The festival boats are decorated with dragons' heads and tails.*

This Chinese dragon boat festival is held in memory of an ancient poet, Qu Yuan, who threw himself off a cliff as a protest against a **corrupt** emperor. The peasants raced to try and save him in their boats, making a great commotion. They threw rice into the water to stop the **demon** fish from eating his body.

Sadly the poet drowned, but he is still remembered every year with this festival. Chinese towns and villages compete against one another in dragon boat races. There is great excitement and noise, with beating drums, gongs, and splashing water.

Making a Dragon Boat

1 Cut the lid and flaps off the box, and decorate it with permanent markers. ▽

You will need:
* Long, thin cardboard box
* Cardboard scraps
* Permanent markers
* Scissors & hole punch
* Glue stick
* Lump clay
* Stick for the sail

2 Fold a large scrap of cardboard in half, and draw a dragon's head on it. Carefully cut it out, making sure you cut through both pieces, but not along the fold. Glue it to the front of the box. ▽

4 Make a hole at the top and bottom of the sail, and thread the stick through. Place the lump of clay in the middle of the box, and push the sail stick in it. ▽

3 Cut out a cardboard square for the sail. Decorate it with the permanent markers. ▷

The dragon boat is ready for racing!

Midsummer Day

△ *Fields of sunflowers grow in the summer sunshine. The sunflowers will then be harvested for their oil.*

Midsummer Day is the longest day of the year in some parts of the world. Many cultures, including the **Incas**, the **Aztecs**, and the **Druids**, worshiped the sun because of the power and strength they believed it gave to the earth. The Inca sun festival, called Inti Raymi, is still held in Peru. A man, dressed as the sun god in a magnificent gold costume, is carried through the streets.

The sunflower has come to **symbolize** the sun, with its round center of closely packed seeds, surrounded by yellow petals that look like the sun's rays.

Making Sunflower Mosaics

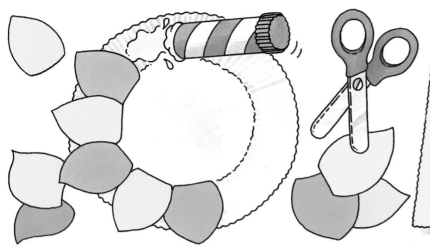

You will need:
* Clean paper plates
* Construction paper scraps
* Scissors and tape
* Glue and brush
* Dried beans and seeds
* Plant sticks
* Flowerpots filled with gravel or stones

1 Cut the petal shapes from yellow paper. Glue them to the edge of the plate with the glue. △

2 Collect some dried beans and seeds, such as peas, lentils, and sunflower seeds. Use them to make a mosaic in the center of the plate, keeping them in place with glue. Let the glue dry. △

3 Carefully turn the sunflower over, and tape the plant stick to the back. Make sure it is very secure. Cut out some leaf shapes and tape them to the sticks. ▽

Make several sunflower mosaics, and plant them in the pots of gravel.

17

Tanabata

The Japanese Star Festival of Tanabata is held in July and celebrates the meeting of the stars of Vega and Altair across the **Milky Way**. During this festival Japanese children write their wishes on paper and tie them to the branches of trees. They hope their wishes will be answered by the stars.

The Japanese have strong beliefs in **astrology** and look to the stars for guidance. Their ancient astrologers believed that the stars could tell them what was going to happen in the future. They knew about the **eclipses** of the sun and moon and the movements of the planets.

At Tanabata a girl ties her paper wish onto a tree branch. ▽

Making Star Wishes

1 Take three bundles of kebab sticks, and arrange them in a triangular shape, as shown. Then tie them together with pieces of colored string. ▽

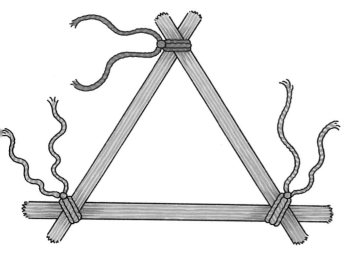

You will need:
* Packet of kebab sticks
* Colored string
* Ribbon
* Construction paper
* Markers

2 Weave in three other bundles of sticks to the first triangle, making a star shape. Tie the sticks together as before, with the colored string. ▽

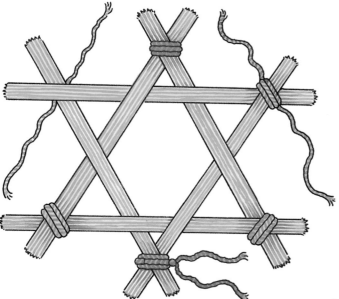

3 Write a secret wish on a small square of construction paper, and fold it up so it cannot be read. Tuck the wish into the star. ▽

4 Make several stars for your friends to put their wishes in. Using pieces of ribbon, tie all the stars to a tree on a starry night. See if your wishes come true. △

Summer Festivals

△ *In Peru the people of Cuzco celebrate midsummer with colorful street parades.*

The summer months are traditionally the most popular time of the year for street festivals in South America and Asia. People dress up in their most colorful costumes. These festivals can be small occasions, when members of a village or a family come together to celebrate a special event, such as a wedding or the birth of a baby.

Whenever groups of people gather together to relax and have fun, there is usually plenty of good food, music, and dancing to enjoy.

Making a Twirling Dancer

1 Draw a spiral shape on the paper. Cut it out around the edge, and decorate it with patterns. △

2 Draw the top half of a dancing figure on the paper, decorate it on both sides, and cut it out. △

3 Cut around the spiral, and make a slit in the center. Make a fold across the waist of the dancer, slide it into the center of the spiral, and tape it in place. △

4 Make a hole in the dancer's head with the needle and attach the thread. Tie the dancer near moving air, and watch her spin and twirl around. ▽

21

Raksha Bandhan

The beautiful festival of Raksha Bandhan is celebrated by most Hindu and Sikh families. One story about this festival explains how the god Indra lost his kingdom to an evil demon, Bali. Indra's wife prayed to the god Vishnu for help, and he gave a bracelet made of braided threads to tie around Indra's wrist. The bracelet protected Indra when he fought the demon Bali again, and he won back his kingdom.

Raksha Bandhan is held on the day of the full moon of Shravana, during July or August. Brothers and sisters exchange promises on this day, and sisters tie a braided bracelet on their brother's wrist.

This sister and brother exchange promises of love and protection. ▽

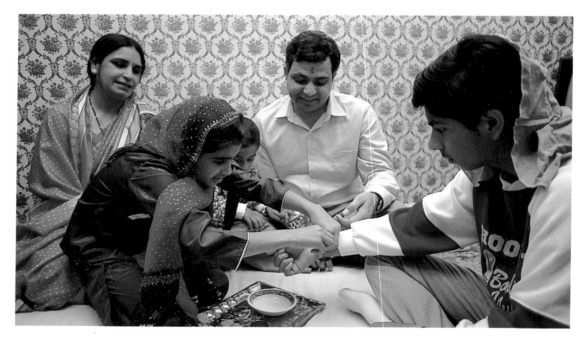

Making Rakhis

You can make colored rakhis by braiding all kinds of wool, thread, and ribbon together. Pipe cleaners are used here because they can be twisted together without braiding.

You will need:
* Colored pipe cleaners
* Ruler and scissors
* Construction paper scraps
* Colored threads
* Needle

1 Take three different colored pipe cleaners. Hold them together tightly, and begin to twist 1 in. from one end. △

2 Continue twisting them together, making the twists as even as possible, until you are about 1 in. from the other end. △

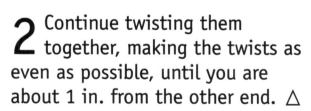

3 Make the pipe cleaners into a bracelet by twisting the two ends together. ▽

Traditionally rakhis are decorated with tassels and charms. Make some shapes from the paper scraps, and tie them to the rakhis.

Summer Sunshine

△ *These children are enjoying an outing on a sunny summer day.*

For many children summertime means a long break from school. People go on trips and take vacations together. Almost everyone is certain to take part in outdoor games, parties, and picnics.

The sun is at its hottest during the summer months. Wearing fewer clothes helps keep you cool, and it is very important to protect your skin from sunburn. It can help to wear a hat to shield your face from the sun. Sunglasses keep the glare of the sun out of your eyes.

Making Snazzy Sunglasses

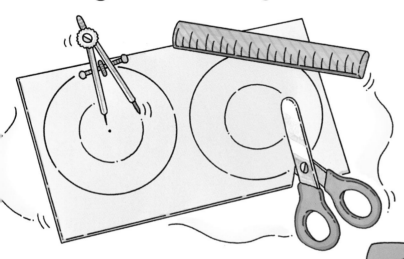

1 Use the compass to draw two circles, 2³/₄ in. diameter, on the paper. Then draw a circle, with a 1 in. diameter, in the center of both. Then cut them out. △

3 You will need to decorate both circles. When they are finished, use the glue stick to glue them to each side of the sunglasses. ▽

2 Cut out shapes from the construction paper to decorate the circles, and stick on colored stickers. Copy the examples here, or think of some of your own ideas. △

Hungry Ghost Festival

◁ *This family has prepared a special meal for its dead relation's "hungry ghost."*

The Hungry Ghost festival is one of the many Chinese celebrations dating back to **ancient** times. It is the custom for Chinese to honor their dead relations and take care of their graves. This Chinese festival, held in August, is a time when spirits of the dead are believed to return and visit their families for thirty days.

During this festival families visit relatives' graves, taking offerings of food. They light sticks of incense and tiny oil lamps to guide the "hungry ghosts" home.

Making Ghost Lanterns

You will need:
* Clean jelly jar
* String
* Tissue paper
* Pencil and scissors
* Tape
* Paints and brush
  Ask an adult to light the candle.

1 The piece of paper will need to be 1 in. wider than the jar so that it is long enough to wrap around. Cut off any extra paper. △

2 Draw the outline of a ghost on the paper, and give it a large mouth. Paint the ghost and let it dry. Cut out the ghost and then the mouth. △

3 Wrap the paper ghost around the jar and tape it in place. Tie a string handle to the rim of the jar. ▷

Ask an adult to place a candle in the jar and to light it. NEVER leave the lanterns unattended when they are lit.

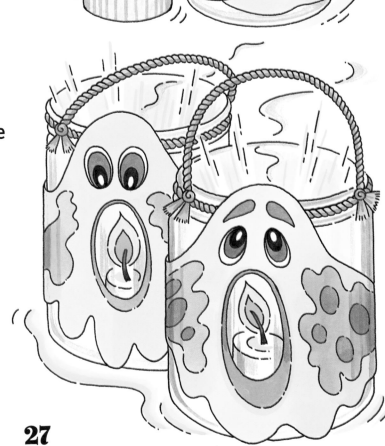

Flower Festivals

Flower festivals are held all over the world during the summer. Some are small events, such as local flower shows. Others, like the Floralies, are much bigger occasions. This festival is held every five years in the city of Ghent, in Belgium. The origin of the Floralies can be traced back to the Roman Floralia, a spring festival held in the honor of the goddess Flora.

Most flowering plants are at their best during the summer months. The colorful flowers attract butterflies and insects, which help **pollinate** the plants.

A spectacular carpet of flowers fills this square in Belgium. ▽

Making a Butterfly Fan

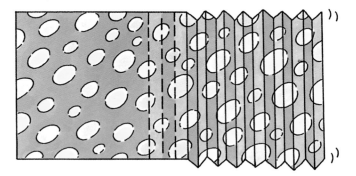

You will need:
* ✳ Colored wrapping paper
* ✳ Ruler
* ✳ Scissors
* ✳ Pipe cleaner
* ✳ Glue stick
* ✳ Two beads
* ✳ Popsicle stick

1 Cut a piece of wrapping paper about 16 x 8 in., and fold it into small pleats. △

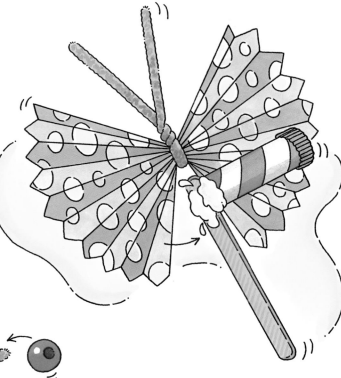

2 Place a pipe cleaner across the middle of the paper. Secure the pleats by twisting the ends of the pipe cleaner together. △

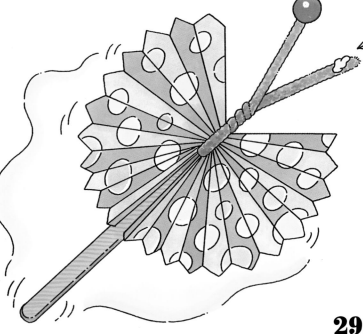

3 Open the folded paper to make a fan. Glue the Popsicle stick to the edges of the fan, using the glue stick. △

4 Put small dabs of glue on the ends of the pipe cleaners and slide a bead onto each side. ◁

Summer Calendar

This calendar refers only to events and festivals mentioned in this book.

May Day and Labor Day
May 1
Beltane
Ancient Celtic Festival
Wesak (Buddhist Festival of Light)
May/June
Tangonosekku (Japanese Boys' Day)
Early May
Kodomonohi (Japanese Children's Day)
Early May
Flag Day
June 14
Independence Day
July 4
Dragon Boat Festival (Chinese Festival)
June
Midsummer's Day
June 21
Tanabata (Japanese Star Festival)
July 7
Raksha Bandhan (Hindu/Sikh Festival)
July or August
Hungry Ghost Festival (Chinese Festival)
August
Floralies (Belgium Flower Festival)
Held every five years during the summer, in Ghent, Belgium

Glossary

adopted To make something or someone belong to you.

ancient Very, very old.

astrology The study of the stars and planets for guidance.

Aztecs Group of people who lived in Mexico before the sixteenth century.

Beltane Old May Day festival celebrated by the Celts.

captive Captured and unable to escape.

Celts A group of people who live in parts of northern Europe.

corrupt When something becomes bad or wicked.

demon A devil or an evil spirit thought to be able to enter a body.

Druids An ancient group of religious people, living in northern Europe.

eclipse A time when a planet, such as the moon, is in a position where it blocks out the sunlight received on Earth.

enlightenment Seeing the truth.

honored Loved, respected, and cared for.

Incas Group of people who lived in South America before the sixteenth century.

Milky Way A group of stars.

original The first.

political Connected to the laws and government of a country.

pollinate To carry pollen from one flower to another.

symbolize To represent something.

Books to Read

Ayer, Eleanor. *Our Flag*. Brookfield, CT: Millbrook Press Inc., 1992.

Gore, Wilma W. *Independence Day*. Springfield, NJ: Enslow Publishers, 1993.

Penney, Sue. *Hinduism*. Discovering Religions. Austin, TX: Raintree Steck-Vaughn, 1997.

Rosen, Mike. *Summer Festivals*. Danbury, CT: Franklin Watts, 1991.

Sandak, Cass. *Patriotic Holidays*. Parsippany, NJ: Silver Burdett Press, 1990.

Webster, David. *Summer*. New York: Simon and Schuster, 1990.

Index